TEXTS FROM DOG

Library of Congress Cataloging-in-Publication Data is available.
ISBN 978-0-544-07774-4

Printed in Mexico
RDT 10 9 8 7 6 5 4 3 2 1

TEXTS FROM DOG

OCTOBER JONES

A Mariner Original ▪ Mariner Books

Houghton Mifflin Harcourt

Boston   New York   2012

INTRODOGTION

HELLO.

My name is Dog, and this book is pretty much all about me.

For boozillions (is that a number?) of years, you humans have been obsessed with dogs. You love us, and we pretend to love you, because you have biscuits and you stroke our bellies like idiots.

We're like BFFs. Best Friends FOREVER.

Now, when human geeks invented the internet in 1811 (I think) it gave you a way to appreciate your Dogs on a WHOLE NEW LEVEL. Oh yes.

Dogs on skateboards. Dogs on surf boards. Singing Dogs. Dancing Dogs. Dogs wearing glasses. Dogs wearing PANTS.

You guys just can't get enough of us...

...Well, guess what?

I'm a Digital Dog in a Digital Age, and I'm pushing the Human/Dog relationship further than it's ever gone before.

How?

I learned a new trick. Yes, siree.

I have a phone, and I'm not afraid to use it.

The following pages are a testament to Dogular intelligence.

A collection of text messages sent from me to my idiot human.

This is the first stage. The next step is canine world domination.

WOOF.

3

Fun day. Ran around the house in a cape. I'M BATDOG LOL

Where did you get the cape?

I think role playing helps alleviate my boredom. I feel so alive x

WHERE DID YOU GET THE CAPE?

I PULLED THE CURTAIN RAIL DOWN. JESUS. WHY CAN'T YOU JUST BE HAPPY FOR ME?

Left phone (12:16) — conversation with "Dog":

So you throw the stick

Yep

I fetch it, and bring it back

Correct

Then what?

I throw it again

What for?

So you can bring it back

SO WHAT THE HELL IS MY MOTIVATION?

Right phone (12:24) — conversation with "Dog":

WHERE IS MR DUCK?

Oh, he's around

Let's make a deal

WHERE IS MR DUCK?

You can have Mr Duck back, if you stop pissing on my bed

LET ME SPEAK TO MR DUCK

QUACK

ARE YOU OK MR DUCK?

He's fine. FOR NOW

8

12

13

14

15

16

WHERE IS MR DUCK?

Under the cupboard in the living room

DON'T PUT HIM UNDER THERE. HE GETS CLAUSTROPHOBIC

It's nice that you care about Mr Duck

IMMA BITE HIS HEAD

Lovely

20

21

22

23

24

25

26

27

28

20:23

Messages **Dog** Edit

Am I a pedigree dog?

Yes

Excellent

If you want, I'll let you kiss my paw

Text Message   Send

29

31

32

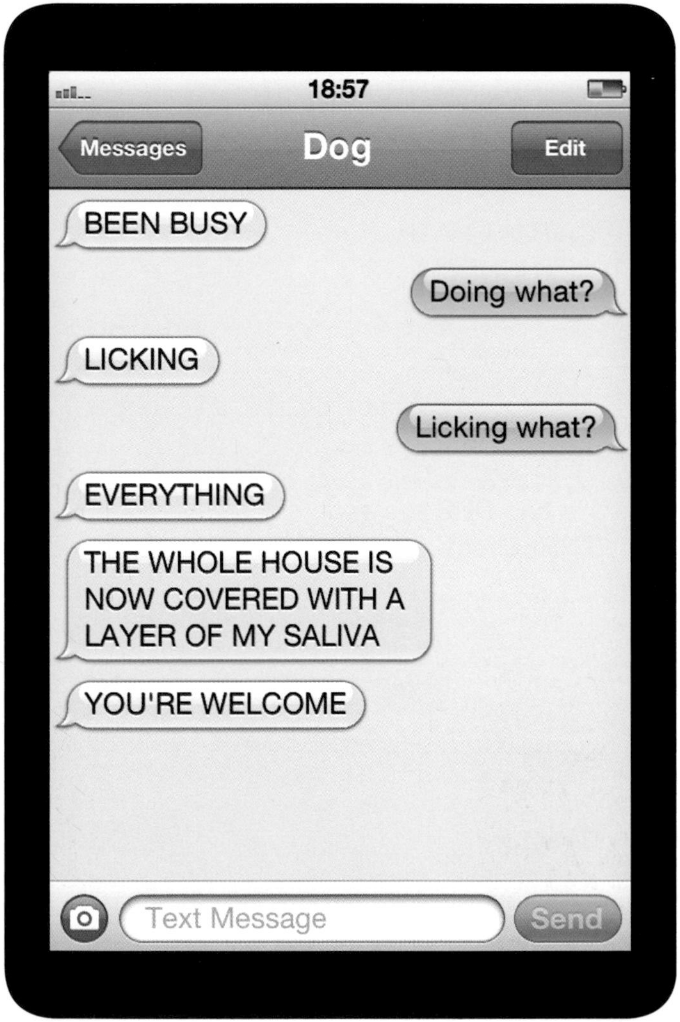
18:57
Messages
Dog
Edit
BEEN BUSY
Doing what?
LICKING
Licking what?
EVERYTHING
THE WHOLE HOUSE IS NOW COVERED WITH A LAYER OF MY SALIVA
YOU'RE WELCOME
Text Message
Send

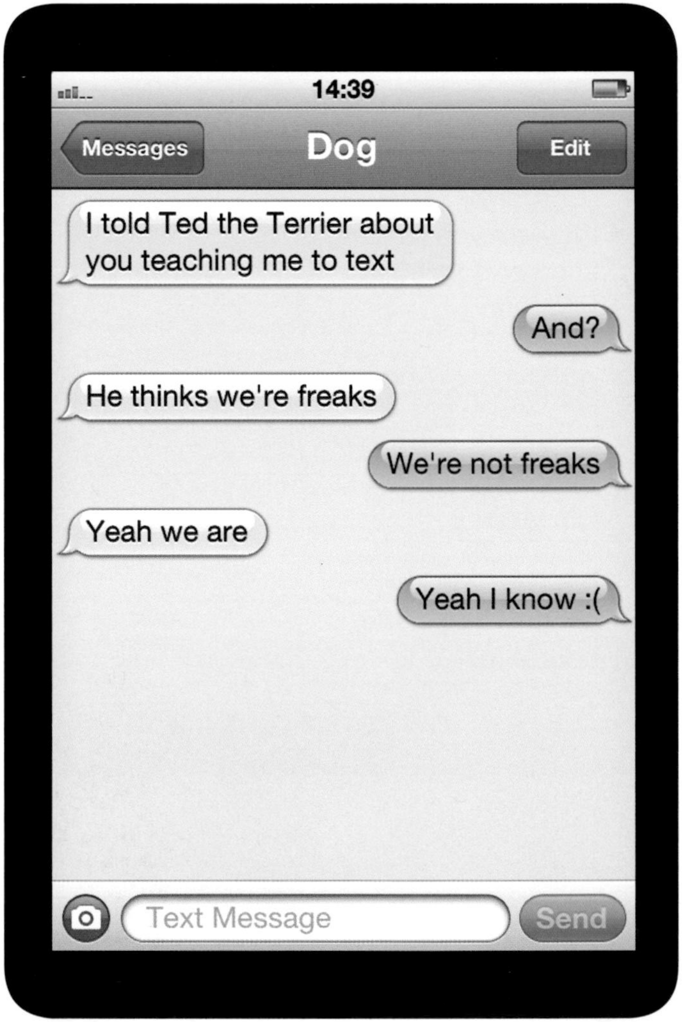
14:39
Messages
Dog
Edit
I told Ted the Terrier about you teaching me to text
And?
He thinks we're freaks
We're not freaks
Yeah we are
Yeah I know :(
Text Message
Send

37

38

39

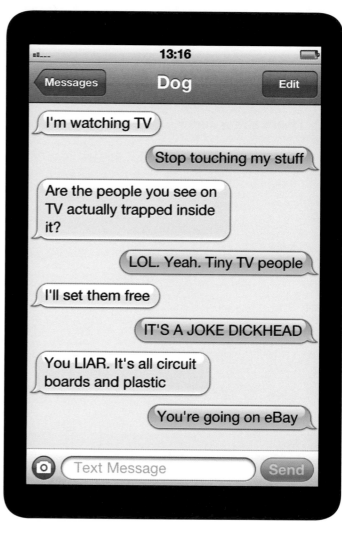

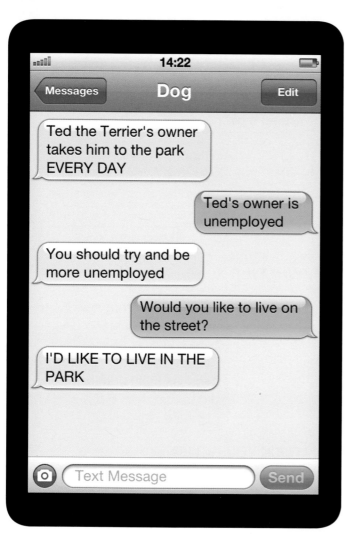

44

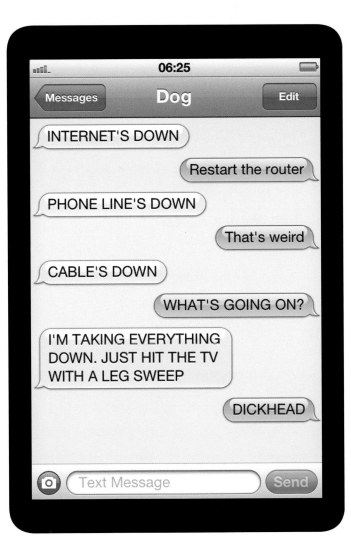

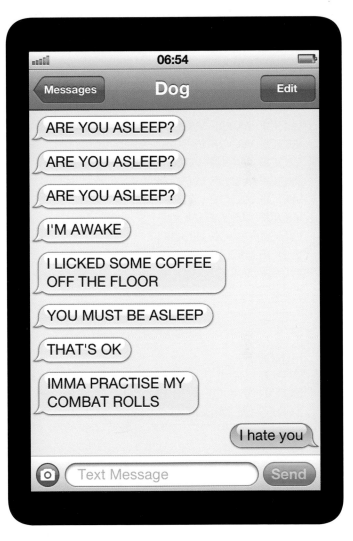

47

49

50

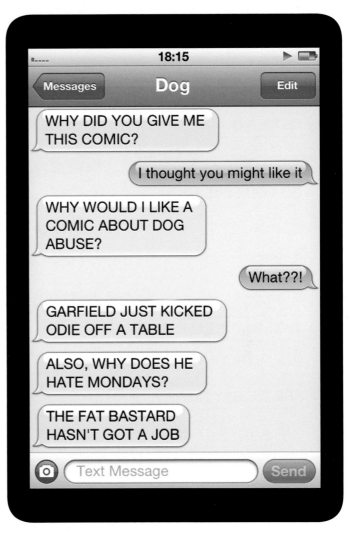

Phone 1 (09:34) — Dog

> I LOVE YOU

Thanks

> DO YOU LOVE ME?

Yep

> SAY IT

Don't be weird

> JUST SAY YOU LOVE ME

I LOVE YOU

> ARE WE GAY NOW?

Phone 2 (22:20) — Dog

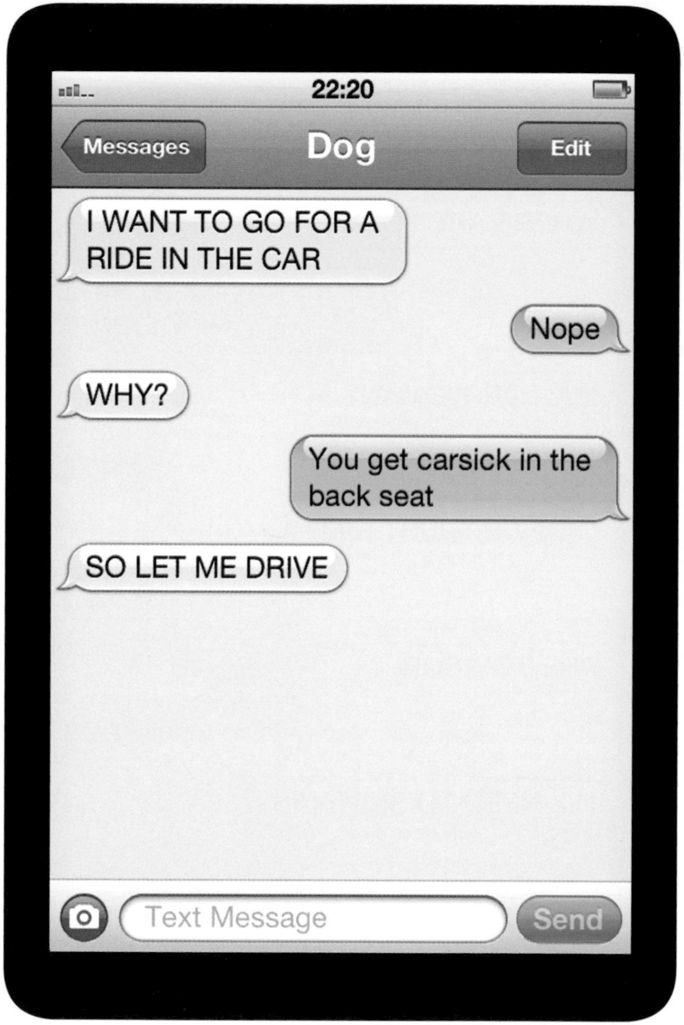

> I WANT TO GO FOR A RIDE IN THE CAR

Nope

> WHY?

You get carsick in the back seat

> SO LET ME DRIVE

54

55

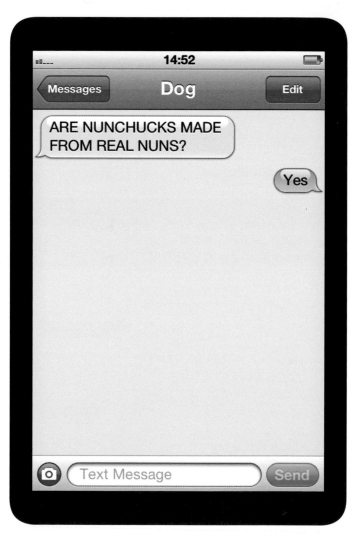

58

59

60

Dog

Just saw this little guy tied up outside a shop

Do you know him?

Yes

I know every dog in the WHOLE WORLD

I sense sarcasm

I sense a DUMBASS

Dog

What kind of dog is Yoda?

Yoda isn't a dog

What is he?

I don't know

So he COULD be a dog

HE'S NOT A DOG

OMG. MAYBE I'M A JEDI

YOU'RE NOT A JEDI

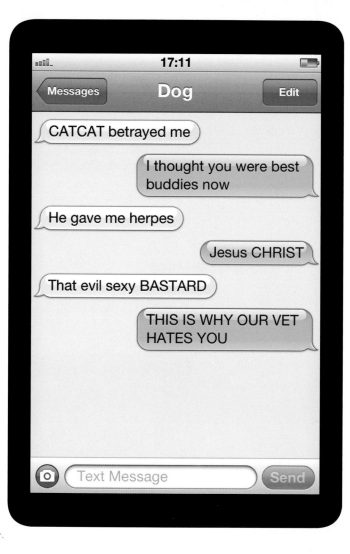

68

70

72

74

75

76

17:01
Messages
Dog
Edit
Are you coming home yet?
No
How about now?
No
How about now?
No
Now?
NO
Now?
Jesus Christ
Text Message
Send

17:15
Messages
Dog
Edit
Now?
NOT YET
How about now?
NOPE
NOW?
NO
When did you leave the house?
8 MINUTES AGO
Will you be back soon?
Text Message
Send

83

88

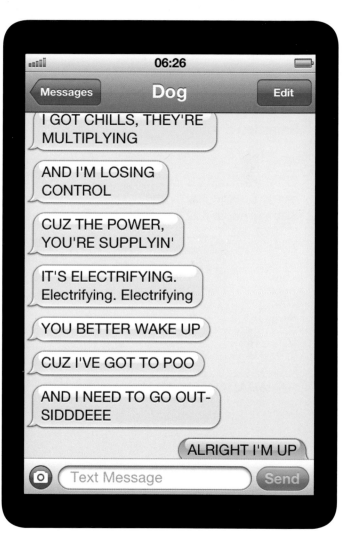

89

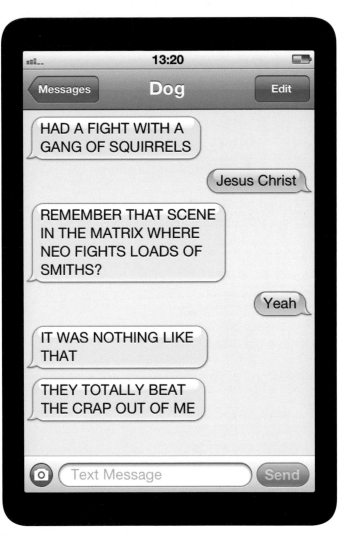

91

92

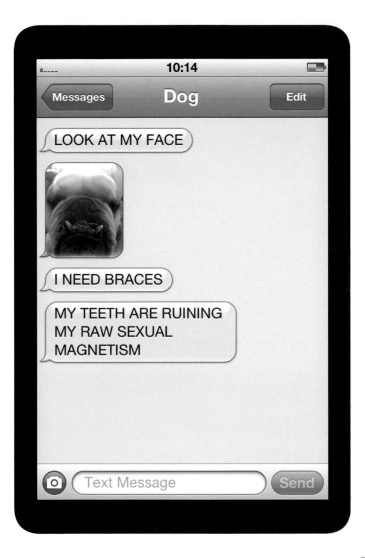

93

94

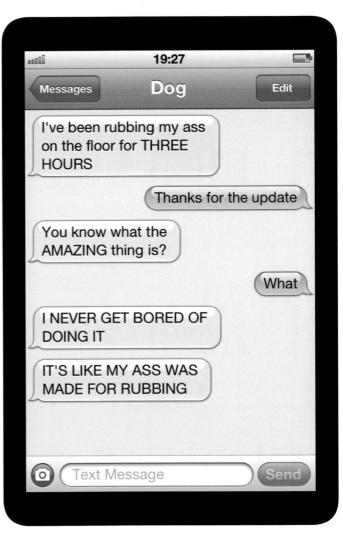

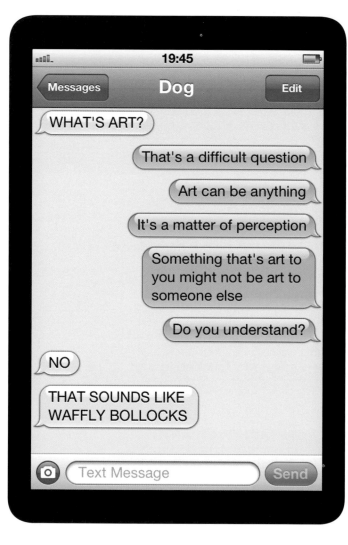

96

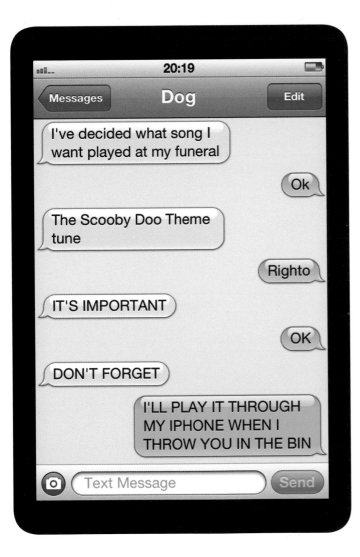

97

Left phone (08:16) — conversation titled "Dog":

ME VS. LASSIE

Lassie

ME VS. SNOOPY

Snoopy

ME VS. THAT WEIRD DOG FROM DILBERT

The one with glasses?

YEAH

He'd kick your ass

Right phone (17:23) — conversation titled "Dog":

Do you think these texts are helping us understand each other better?

Yes

I'm totally awesome

You're a total douche

Good talk

DOG & I

OCTOBER JONES was born and raised in Birmingham, England, where, ironically, he spent most of his childhood terrified of dogs. He has recently worked on animation projects for the BBC, as well as doing music videos for UK comedy band The Amateur Transplants.

DOG is the runt of a five-puppy litter born on a farm in Wales. He was the last to be sold, and arrived in Birmingham slighted and grouchy. He spends most of his time napping, snacking, trying to figure out who the second dog in the bedroom mirror is, and, of course, texting.